Ab▐ ‖‖‖‖‖‖‖‖‖‖‖‖‖‖‖‖‖‖‖‖
D1362584

EASTON

First published in 2014 by Wayland
Text copyright © Wayland 2014
Illustrations © Wayland 2014

Wayland
338 Euston Road
London NW1 3BH

Wayland Australia
Level 17/207 Kent Street
Sydney, NSW 2000

The rights of Tom Easton to be identified as the Author
and Sophie Escabasse to be identified as the Illustrator of this
Work have been asserted by them in accordance with the
Copyright, Designs and Patents Act, 1988.

Series Editor: Victoria Brooker
Series design: Robert Walster and Basement68
Consultant: Dee Reid

A CIP catalogue record for this book is available
from the British Library.
Dewey number: 823.9'2-dc23

ISBN 978 0 7502 8225 3
eBook ISBN: 978 0 7502 8565 0

2 4 6 8 10 9 7 5 3 1

Printed in China

Wayland is a division of Hachette Children's Books,
an Hachette UK Company
www.hachette.co.uk

Dig It

Tom Easton and Sophie Escabasse

WAYLAND
www.waylandbooks.co.uk

Miss Collins is the Careers Officer.
She's been fixing up work experience
for me.

"I have a new job for you," she said.

"Not sweeping the yard at the
Rubbish Tip," I said. "Please!"

"Not the job at the Rubbish Tip," Miss Collins said. She handed me a card.

"Grave digger!" I yelped.

"It's that or the Rubbish Tip," she replied.

"I can dig," I said quickly.

The man at the graveyard handed
me a spade.

"Dig," he said, pointing.
The man's name was John.
He didn't talk much.

I dug. It was boring. I wasn't
thinking about what I was doing.
I forgot to stop.

John came back.

He looked over the edge of the hole.

Maybe it was a bit deep.

John got a ladder. He helped me out.

John pointed again.
This time to a little shed.

"There are 6 coffins in there," John said. "Dig 6 holes for them. Just 6 feet deep."

John pointed to the hole I'd dug.

"Fill that in until it's only 6 feet deep," he said.

I sighed. This was going to take days.

"You need to finish before you go home," he said.

My mouth dropped.

"But I have football practice at 6!" I said.

"Sorry," he said. John walked off.
I thought about just leaving.
It's not as if I was getting paid.

But I knew John would write a report.
I couldn't get into more trouble.
Not after last time.

17

I looked at the coffins.
I looked at the hole.
I looked at my watch.
I had an idea.

Then the third and the fourth.
Then the fifth.

The last coffin poked out the top
a bit. I covered it over with earth.
It looked OK.

I used more soil to make six mounds. When I had finished, they all looked the same.

I threw the shovel down.

I wiped my hands on my jeans.

I smiled at how clever I was.

John would be pleased, I thought.

But John wasn't pleased.

"Where are the coffins?" he asked.

"Where are the holes?"

"The coffins are in the holes,"
I said. I smiled proudly.
"I've buried them."

John looked like he wanted to put me in a hole.

"We're supposed to bury them all tomorrow," he said. "When their families are here!"

"Now you tell me," I said.

John handed me the shovel.

"Get digging," he said.

It looked like I wasn't going
to football practice after all.

Read more stories about Dan.

978 0 7502 8228 4

Dan's latest work experience is at a car yard. All Dan has to do is sell a car. What could possibly go wrong?

978 0 7502 8226 0

Dan's latest work experience is at a flower shop. All Dan has to do is deliver flowers on Valentine's Day. What could possibly go wrong?

978 0 7502 8227 7

Dan's latest work experience is at a radio station. All Dan has to do is mop floors. What could possibly go wrong?

Read some more books in the Freestylers series.

FOOTBALL FACTOR

Each story follows the ups and downs of one member of the football team Sheldon Rovers as they aim for Cup glory.

978 0 7502 7985 7

978 0 7502 7980 2

978 0 7502 7982 6

978 0 7502 7984 0

978 0 7502 7981 9

978 0 7502 7983 3

SHORT THRILLERS

Cool crime detectives, Jas and Sam, solve spine-chilling cases with humour and bravery.

978 0 7502 6895 0

978 0 7502 6896 7

978 0 7502 6898 1

978 0 7502 6897 4

FOR TEACHERS

About Freestylers

Freestylers is a series of carefully levelled stories, especially geared for struggling readers. With very low reading age and high interest age, these books are humorous, fun, up-to-the-minute and edgy. Core characters provide familiarity in all of the stories, build confidence and ease pupils from one story through to the next, accelerating reading progress.

Freestylers can be used for both guided and independent reading. To make the most of the books you can:

- Focus on making each reading session successful. Talk about the text before the pupil starts reading. Introduce the characters, the storyline and any unfamiliar vocabulary.

- Encourage the pupil to talk about the book during reading and after reading. How would they have felt if they were one of the characters? How would they have dealt with the situations that Dan found himself in?

- Talk about which parts of the story they like best and why.

For guidance, this story has been approximately measured to:

National Curriculum Level: 2C   ATOS: 1.5
Reading Age: 6   Lexile ® Measure [confirmed]: 170L
Book Band: Orange